D1488564

Panties

Panties

A brief history

Sarah Tomczak
& Rachel Pask

First published in the United States by DK Publishing, Inc., 375 Hudson Street New York, New York 10014

A CIP catalogue for this book is available from the Library of Congress.
ISBN 0 7566 0757 4

Conceived and produced by Elwin Street Limited
79 St John Street
London EC1M 4NR
www.elwinstreet.com

Designer: Simon Osborne
Editor: Debbie Foy
Photographer: Noam Toran

Printed and bound in Singapore
987654321

Contents

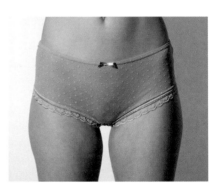

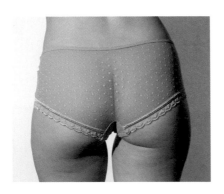

Introduction: A Brief Affair

If Marilyn Monroe happened to be standing on a subway grate and the wind whipped up her white dress, what underwear would be revealed? Simple, snug briefs? Men's boxer shorts? A red lace thong? With so many choices out there, the knickers that cover a woman's most intimate bits can reveal more than you realize. Lingerie is a glimpse into a woman's secret self; the person she is underneath the layers of clothes and who she becomes when the lights go out.

Knickers, panties, bloomers, briefs – call them what you will – but just feel lucky to wear a different pair every day. Only high society had the luxury of daily underwear changes 200 years ago, and for many years before that, men were the sole pant-wearers – leaving women to feel the breeze.

But let's look back even further in time, to the first reported sightings of smalls. Picture this: Ancient Egypt 3,000 B.C., a stylish Sumerian girl knots her cloth between her legs, creating the first makeshift pair of briefs. The Egyptian people are so impressed with this fashion-forward statement that they immortalize the girl in terracotta and this Babylonian babe can now be viewed at the Louvre, in Paris.

Several hundred years later Greek frescoes confirmed the existence of underwear by revealing women wearing foundation undergarments (the first power pants!) and athletic briefs. By the fourth century, ankle-length pants had become common-place – but not for women. These bloomers were deemed unfeminine, leaving women no other choice but to go the way of Sharon Stone in *Basic Instinct* and omit them altogether.

By the 1800s, knitted drawers were *de rigueur* for both sexes. And once women were finally given the chance to cover themselves, there was no holding them back. From humble muslin underpants came a treasure trove of gorgeous underthings. Old-style silk bloomers gave way to power pants; classic cotton to racy, lacy thongs and G-strings.

Undies have always caused a scandal, and this tome reveals the juiciest ones – from the sports star who made the front page of the national papers five days in a row thanks to her choice of knickers, to the supermodel whose ad campaign for her lingerie line was banned because the pictures were just too intimate.

You'll also find inside info on the origins of all the favorite pant styles; you'll discover which screen stars became infamous because of their smalls, and which celebrities are desperate to deck out every girl's booty. You'll learn about the past, present, and future of hot bot fashion; from lace to leather, boy shorts to bikini briefs. This book is your guide to the gorgeous world of panties. So join us as we embark on a journey into the depths of a woman's underwear drawer . . .

Old School Glamor

Silk underwear has always been synonymous with high-class refinement. While peasants made do with chafing, ragged cotton, the upper echelons of Victorian society were the first to use this rich, buttery-soft fabric to transform their underwear.

. . . . . ● . . . . .

Nowadays we prefer our smalls to be . . . well, miniscule, but circa 1880, the bigger the pant, the better. If you hoisted the petticoats of a classy lady, you'd find a pair of enormous, blousy shorts that fell below the knee, but in an ironic twist for this overly moral era, each leg was separate (they tied together at the waist). Easy access? The aristocracy may have pretended to be demure, but these open-crotched panties surely fueled the frolicking on the chaise-lounge before afternoon tea was served. And the nineteenth-century peep-show "What the Butler Saw," with its saucy flashes of boobs and bums glimpsed by the hired help, got its inspiration from somewhere . . .

For the record, the Victorians claimed the open-crotch design was all about hygiene and that the wind whistling around their nether regions would keep things as fresh as a daisy, despite their infrequent underwear changes.

But it's not just the slipperiness of the silk that makes this style of panties so arousing, it's all the adornments: lacy edges that frame your undulations, covered buttons crying out to be undone, a little ribbon to untie, some strategically placed embroidery – and we've got the Victorians to thank for that, too. Imagine an exquisite pair of black silk knickers edged with ecru lace and a baby-pink ribbon. A creation of the ultra-risqué, London-based lingerie designers

Agent Provocateur, you think? Nope, this is Victorian handiwork, circa 1905. If you don't believe me, check out the fashion history department of a good museum.

No wonder the Victorians snagged the French term "lingerie" to describe women's smalls – with designs that exhibited so much more *je ne sais quoi* than the highly functional title "underwear." Silk panties were responsible for putting sexy underwear on the map. But what became of the split crotch? It hung around until the 1930s – when, finally, stitched-up knickers became the only thing to wear and men everywhere wiped the tears from their eyes.

The Victorians claimed the open-crotch design was all about hygiene: the wind rushing around the nether regions would keep things fresh as a daisy.

Surprisingly, it was the racy Parisian cancan dancers that finally sent split knickers to their grave. While these femmes fatales preferred to retain some of their dignity, they also caused a storm by chopping their long, blousy knickers super short to reveal more thigh during those high-leg kicks than ever before. And here are knickers as we know them – with that French moniker, courtesy of the cabaret girls who knew how to start a trend.

For a while, shortie knickers were the only thing to wear under your girdle – the Twenties' flappers loved them because the new shorter style of pants worked with knee-length skirts and resembled men's briefs (those girls were all about androgyny), but even the more feminine of women were lured in by their elegance and versatility. Genevieve Antoine Dariaux, the famed fashion author, noted in her book, *Elegance,* that the height of sophistication in the Thirties was

to match your innerwear to your outerwear, and so briefs became available in a multitude of shades, such as sky, mauve, coral, lemon, champagne, and cyclamen.

French silk knickers seem incomplete without a scarlet mouth and Lana Turner waves. The epitome of old Hollywood glamor, when you picture a pair, they're usually covering the perfect posterior of a 1940s movie star. These screen sirens also helped the craze for cami-knickers (a union of camisole and knickers) reach an all-time high. Think Claudette Colbert in *It Happened One Night* or Betty Grable in *Pin-Up Girl,* wearing silk slips and French knickers that whispered naughtily of sexual

Below: 1920s actress Hope
Hampton displays the latest
Parisian fashion: ruffled bloomers.

PARISIAN INSPIRATIONS
IN COLOUR
Displayed by
HOPE HAMPTON

promise. These were women with killer figures, but with the Hays code in place – a law that banned skin-bearing booty shots – French knickers were as raunchy as it got. With no room for Britney-esque navel-baring or Pammy Anderson-style cleavage, Hollywood kept us horny with body-clinging silks and satins instead. But don't you agree that a pert, rounded buttock, brushing up against taut, silky fabric is way more tantalizing than an in-your-face full butt flash?

Without the funds of an A-list movie star, women who were hooked on silk smalls had to be crafty; they splashed out on the fabric and stitched their own patterns. Even World War II rationing couldn't stand between the girls and their coveted undergarments. Savvy seamstresses were only too happy to intensify foreign relations with homesick American airmen, who were, in turn, only too happy to spare a little parachute silk for the right gal with the wrong morals.

The girl who fills her underwear drawer with silk lingerie is a romantic at heart.

Legend has it that it was the actions of a quick-thinking jezebel that first gave rise to the word "parachute." In 1916 a certain married English lord met with a French lady of high class and extraordinary beauty while on a military excursion with the Royal Flying Corps in France. They fell passionately in love and the following year, unable to bear the separation from his French mistress any longer, the lord insisted that she visit him at his castle in Yorkshire. The lovers were celebrating their reunion when the lord's disgruntled wife, brandishing her husband's dueling pistols, disturbed them. In a moment of panic and inspiration, the Gallic libertine leapt from the bedroom window using her finest silk bloomers as a canopy to ease the speed of her fall, landing unscathed on the far side of the moat. Having survived the wrath of his spouse, and ever the practical man, the amorous aristocrat pioneered the use of silk as a canopy material. Wishing to acknowledge his French lover's ingenuity, but without jeopardizing her honor, he christened his innovation the parachute – a combination of the French words *para*, "protection against," and *chute*, "fall."

Today, these passionate panties are still as hip as ever. Sure, the underwear market has been bombarded with new shapes and styles, but none have the class and caché of French knickers. Though it's over 60 years since the stars of the big screen first whetted our appetites, women still succumb to the allure of these smalls. Wearing these sexy silks makes a woman feel grown-up and ladylike, with poise and elegance. The girl who fills her underwear drawer with silk lingerie is a romantic at heart; a retro girl, who's charmed by the thought of a bygone era and still holds out hope for a Cary Grant of her own. She's whimsical, extravagant, and, above all, exceptionally classy.

If a woman feels like a flashback she can buy her own original silk knickers from a vintage store. Websites and specialty boutiques offer new, never-been-worn garments from the last century. (Expect them to be more expensive the more "vintage" they are).

The champagne brand of the underwear world, La Perla, is the place to head for classic silk panties. This Italian underwear mecca simply oozes sophistication, imparting an air of affluence that stays with the shopper when they leave the store clutching their beautifully wrapped smalls. Their finely cut lingerie is the epitome of elegance and femininity, but just when you thought silk couldn't get any more

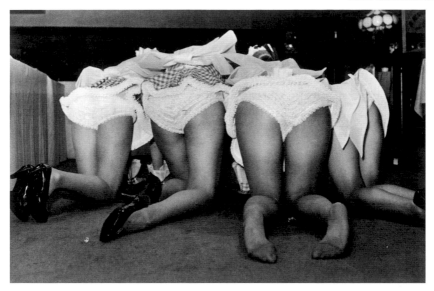

seductive, La Perla make their vintage-inspired styles quite literally
sex on legs by snapping them on exquisite models draped over leather
sofas wearing only damp hair, glowing skin, fuchsia stilettos, and
"come hither" expressions.

Emerging during the strictly moral Victorian era, silk knickers
have managed to combine discretion and seduction. See them as
the Swiss finishing school of the underwear world: elegant, proper,
and refined – yet they're also impromptu semi-striptease, as it takes
only one gust of wind to make that floaty fabric fly up and a woman
is flashing to the world. Silk pants are the epitome of French fancy –
stylish, sensuous, and spontaneously saucy. Slip on a pair for a little
joie de vivre.

RIGBY & PELLER

Back when underwear was known as "unmentionables,"
Mrs B. Rigby and Mrs G. Peller established a company that
became famous for its made-to-measure corsetry and lingerie.
So much so that even Her Majesty wanted a piece of the action.

These days, royals from home and abroad, and stars from the big and small screens, are regulars at the classy Rigby & Peller establishment. Surprisingly for a store that supplies smalls to the rich and famous, the briefs are reasonably priced, with the cheapest pair selling for under £15 ($27); mere pocket money for HRH. Thongs have flown off the shelves recently, with R&P's own brand and Prima Donna being the favorite labels. However, trends have no place in the rigidly traditional R&P. "We buy what sells, not what's in fashion or what we like," says Operations Director, Jill Kenton.

When celebrities visit the store at the weekend they are shuffled through to avoid the normal two-hour wait. Home visits are for the select few. Jill fits Cherie Blair, the Prime Minister's wife, at No. 10 Downing Street three times a year, while her mother, June, fits the Queen. Some few years ago, Jill and June had lunch at Kensington Palace with Princess Diana; butler Paul Burrell was serving.

R&P's profile keeps rising and their panties make an appearance in the *Bridget Jones's Diary* sequel: *The Edge of Reason*. With interest growing from both sides of the Atlantic, what does the future hold for R&P? "We'll stick to what we know," they reply, sagely. Wise words, since R&P customers tend to be customers for life.

Classic Cotton

Cotton briefs – in their own unconcerned way – are really quite sexy. Pure and natural, they are like a woman without make-up. Stripped of frills, lace, and peepholes, but boasting comfortable fabric and a generous cut, they are the classic, everyday brief.

· · · · ● ● ● · · ·

The woman who chooses cotton panties is a no-nonsense kinda gal. She knows what she likes and she's not impressed or seduced by expensive fabrics or elaborate designs. For her, underwear has a job to do and she's not going to spend a fortune on a basic pair of knickers when she can buy them in a three-pack from her local department store with her lunch money.

On the one hand, cotton knickers can be seen as incredibly average, perhaps even boring, but at the same time they have a wonderfully wholesome image that men can't seem to resist. Is it the virginal aspect of these panties? The crisp, white cotton whispers purity and modesty; it's as if removing them would be like doing so for the first time ever . . . Or, perhaps it's their retro simplicity – reminiscent of a golden age before the underwear market became saturated with spandex thongs – when all a gorgeous girl wore was cotton briefs. If you imagine a 1970s shampoo commercial, a girl in pure, white knickers (visible through her gauzy sundress) running through a cornfield with her flaxen mane flying out around her, then you have a measure of just how sexy cotton panties can be.

The Sixties was the decade that cotton briefs were coronated as the ruler of the underwear kingdom. "Teenagers" were new in town – until then, there had been no such thing as adolescents. Now a whole

new generation emerged and these young women wanted to differentiate themselves from their curvy, girdle-wearing mothers. These girls preferred denim pedal-pushers to pencil skirts and pearls, and wore their briefs in basic cotton instead of the fancy silks and nylons their mother's favored. Young was "in" and shopping in London's hip new Kings Road stores was all the rage. With the opening of high-fashion boutiques like Mary Quant and Biba came the trend for miniskirts, requiring panties to be super-short and skimpy.

It was around 1967 that the longer-style briefs (which sat high on the waist and came mid-way down the thigh) got the chop and teens started to shop for the same "bikini-style" briefs that we wear today. Sixties British icon Twiggy liked her smalls . . . well, small, and as with everything the diminutive supermodel did, the public soon followed.

Think of cotton briefs like a woman without make-up – pure, natural, and fuss-free.

Hippies also found peace, love, and harmony in cotton – after all, it was nature's fabric – and while the flower-power kids were burning their bras and chanting of free love, cotton underpants were still their underwear of choice.

The Seventies saw men's and women's fashions converge (for some reason, everyone wanted to be seen in flares), so underwear styles became androgynous and both sexes soon found themselves in identical his 'n' hers cotton smalls. These briefs kept everyone happy. They were cheaper to produce than silk or satin, therefore affordable to everyone; they were comfortable to wear; and the natural, breathable fabric made them the healthy choice. Department stores soon cornered the craze and started to sell the "can't get enough of 'em" pants in packs of three, five, or even seven (one for every day of the week.) Females from the ages of 5 to 95 could wear these briefs, and they did.

Forget frumpiness, the right pair of cotton briefs became a sexual metaphor for the kind of woman you were, or wanted to be. Lace was obvious – the wearer was a blatant sex goddess – but cotton was subtle. The kind of woman who chose them pretended to be pure, but you'd never know if she was burning with lust under the surface. Peeling off those cool, white panties could unleash a red-hot woman within.

Although they are the classic brief, cotton panties have also moved with the times. Back in the Seventies, briefs were cut low, like the hipster flares worn on top, but the butt was fully covered. Jump forward a decade and with Eighties fashion in full throttle, knickers got a drastic makeover. Women were suddenly more body-conscious and bitten by the workout bug. To show off some skin, legs were cut higher and higher, a thick waistband finished above the navel and the butt cheeks got a little less coverage. This new style rocked beaches and aerobics classes all over the western world and can be seen in its full glory in the classic Eighties movie *Flashdance*, where Jennifer Beal – welder by day, dancer by night – leaps and bounds in high-cut cotton briefs, perfecting her dance routines and attempting to live out her dreams.

Are you a red-hot woman beneath those cotton briefs?

Dance diva Jennifer Lopez paid homage to these infamous dance scenes in *Flashdance* for her single "I'm Glad" but, sadly, she replaced Beal's high-cut briefs with a pair of low-cut boy-style briefs with fuller coverage over the butt, which are more popular today.

THE POSTMAN ALWAYS RINGS TWICE

Director: Bob Rafelson, 1981

The Postman Always Rings Twice **rubs shoulders with the likes of** *Caligula, 9½ Weeks,* **and** *Basic Instinct* **as one of the films in the top ten list of steamy movie moments.**

And what makes it so hot? A certain scene where Cora (Jessica Lange) gives her husband's employee, Frank (Jack Nicholson), a flash of her cotton panties, which tips him over the edge. The scene where his head is wedged firmly between her legs while he relieves her of her underwear was considered so hot that it was censored.

But for a matter of months, it could easily have been Meryl Streep showing off her smalls on the big screen. She was first choice for the role in the 1981 movie remake, but was pregnant at the time (clearly maternity pants didn't hold the same appeal), so Jessica Lange struck lucky

and landed the part of sexy femme fatale. Nicholson had been impressed with her role in *King Kong*, but before the picture began he was keen to discuss the technical aspects of the film. "It was my obligation to know that when we're in the middle of a multimillion-dollar movie no one gets shy," he explained. "So I asked her a lot of questions – how she felt about nudity and playing skin-to-skin intimate scenes." Clearly it wasn't an issue.

Lange's knicker-flashing scene has caught the imagination of US-based sex expert Julia Mason. She advises couples to spice up boring nookie by acting out steamy scenes from hit

movies. Her new study, called "Making Love Like Hollywood", gives dozens of couples hot movie homework projects, and 90 percent of the participants agreed that replaying the starring roles is a massive turn-on.

As for Jessica Lange, she hasn't shied away from intimate scenes since. She recently starred in the movie *Big Fish*, during which she shared a romantic moment in a bathtub. "Sexuality or sensuality of some type is usually tied in to the emotional life of my characters," she admitted. Although she kept her knickers on this time around.

It's funny to think that a fabric first used worldwide in 1500 still has the underwear market cornered today. Now cotton briefs are available in almost every style and colour under the sun. From thongs to bikini briefs, boyshorts to granny pants. And if you think there's nothing luxurious about cotton, think again.

Designers have made their mark on the industry, and now the same fashion house that created your skirt, stilettos, and sunglasses will also provide you with snazzy designer smalls. And who doesn't want to look like Kate Moss in her Calvin Klein briefs?

In fact, in the battle of the sexes, it's no longer a question of who wears the trousers, but who's wearing the boxers or Y-fronts beneath them. Forget serious cross-dressing, we're talking more Annie Hall than *Boys Don't Cry*. The women who shun a frilly little thong in favor of a pair of sturdy boxers are totally in touch with their femininity. In fact they're so savvy when it comes to their own sexual allure, these girls know that displaying their curves in a pair of men's undies is far more of a turn-on than any obvious and contrived lace creation.

And so, even today, cotton panties continue to be a contradiction – a basic choice that women make for comfort and cost – with little attention to sexual appeal, yet at the same time fantasy fodder for men, and a symbol of purity just waiting to be sullied . . . The question is – are you a red-hot woman beneath those cotton briefs?

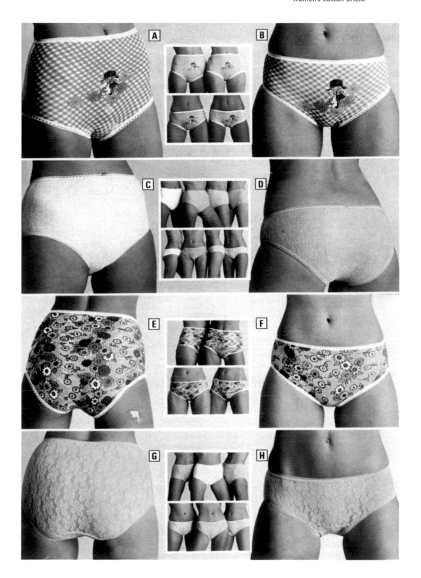

In the battle of the sexes,
it's not a question of who wears
the trousers, but who's wearing
the boxers beneath them.

BONDS

If you ever thought there weren't big bucks to be made in cotton undies, Aussie brand Bonds has proven otherwise. Their low-rise hipster pants have turned into an AUD$6.5 million business in the space of a mere two years.

Since the launch of the 1999 collection, Bonds can make the extraordinary claim that they have sold the equivalent of 10 pairs of undies to every Australian woman. They can also boast that they were the originators of the hipster shape which is now flying off shelves all over the world. Kelly Osbourne and Britney Spears both swear by the brand, but exactly how did the trend begin?

Cotton hipsters became mainstream when the big wigs at Bonds spotted a gap in the market. General Manager Sue Morphet noticed that if you were female, aged thirty-plus, and looking for a decent pair of knickers, the contemporary offering of granny pants and micro G-strings didn't really hit the mark. Hence the brand went back to the drawing board, came up with a whole new design and told these women nationwide to kiss their G-strings goodbye.

Cue the launch of the hipster Bonds Boxer, which comes in a traditional loose style and also in a cheeky tighter fit. The wildly successful ad campaigns feature model Sarah O'Hare lolling about the house parodying male slobbiness.

But Bonds didn't stop there. Unsatisfied with revolutionizing female underwear, Bonds dabbled with men's undies. Determined for guy's cotton pants to be as gorgeous as the girls,

the brand declared an "Undie Amnesty." At a number of venues Bonds gave men the chance to swap their gray, faded Y-fronts for some hipster trunks or "guyfronts," and girlfriends all over the southern hemisphere rejoiced. Stretching their talents across the pond, Bonds have recently started selling a range at the UK high street stores Top Shop, House of Fraser, and Selfridges.

Sports Briefs

Sports briefs are hard for the sexes to agree on. While women have disturbing memories of struggling into these nylon horrors in the girls' locker room, men have managed to create an entire erotic mystique around the very same underthings.

Despite the fact that the sexy-popular-girls-semi-naked-in-the-locker-room scene is an essential component of any teen movie, the sad truth is that sports underwear just isn't that hot. Generally made of Aertex or a breathable nylon, these panties are meant to hold everything in – and hide it from prying eyes, too. Whereas most styles of modern lingerie are designed to show the wearer at her sexiest, these underpants have been created to protect her modesty and hide anything that could be glimpsed under that impossibly short skirt. Yet the combination of a flirty, pleated mini, flying up to reveal a good solid pair of knickers is strangely arousing in itself, which could explain why these panties are a uniform staple of cheerleaders, netball players, and tennis stars. (Haven't these people heard of shorts? But would they have so many spectators if they had?)

Tennis was one of the birthplaces of the sports brief, particularly when adorning the rear of one of its stars, "Gorgeous Gussy Moran." The American honey chose the 1949 Wimbledon Championships to debut a pair of lace-trimmed panties under her white skirt. Move over Janet Jackson, Moran's "wardrobe malfunction" made the front page of the U.K.'s *Daily Express* five times in one week, but she wasn't thrilled with the publicity. "After the lace panties, everyone was always staring to see what I was wearing and I couldn't concentrate on my tennis," she said.

But Moran can't take total credit for the fashion moment. The designer of the lacy sports panties was Teddy Tinling, a former umpire-turned-couturier, with an eye for a trend. His designs may have caused a scandal back in the day, but since then, tennis stars like Mary Lou Retton and Annabel Croft have paid homage to Tinling with their own frilly briefs. Embracing the publicity, the designer tried his luck again 10 years later when he created a pair of gold lamé panties for tennis star Karol Fagero. Wimbledon banned them before they even made it onto court.

Generally speaking, sport has played a big part in the development of underwear. If it wasn't for the sudden Victorian enlightenment that exercise promoted good health, women would all be standing around *sans* panties. To be able to work up a sweat, women had to ditch some of the petticoats and don knickers instead – to be worn while walking, golfing, or horse-riding.

The combination of a flirty, pleated mini, flying up to reveal a good solid pair of knickers is strangely arousing.

The knock-on effect means women are now able to sport spandex shorts for their Pilates, spinning, and kickboxing classes.

But getting women to lose the layers and choose the type of underwear worn predominantly by men was a slow process, and it was another American, Amelia Bloomer, who attempted to speed things up. In 1851, the journalist herself arrived on UK soil intending to promote her new invention – baggy drawers that tied at the ankle, specially developed for sport. They were called "Bloomers." It took about 50 years for women to take her seriously, but eventually her glorious knickerbockers gained a following and made it into the history books.

"BLOOMERISM,"
OR THE
NEW FEMALE COSTUME OF 1851,

As it has appeared in the various Cities and Towns.

BOSTON: S. W. WHEELER, 66 Cornhill—1851.

"You can call her an outdoor girl if she has the bloom of youth on her cheeks and the cheeks of youth in her bloomers."
—Anon

Women should rejoice that they have the option of underwear created solely for sport; be happy that they have the choice of changing into *anything* while doing their sporting activity. As late as the 1960s, British pupils in school gym classes were expected to strip down to their pants and vest to climb the monkey bars and walk the beam, until Aertex was invented and the country went barmy for this breathable fabric. From then on, schools insisted that all pupils should have a gym kit made from the wonder weave.

Like all panties, sports briefs have inched smaller and smaller over the years. Amelia Bloomer would shudder at the sight of the super-hero-inspired, thong-worn-over-tights fashion of the middle Eighties – including actress Jane Fonda and singer Sheena Easton. Suddenly, fitness tapes were all the rage, and in the body-conscious era of *Baywatch* babes, the sports thong had a definite appeal. Nowadays sport and sex appeal go hand-in-hand with athletes keeping it brief – and hot. Track stars like Florence Griffith Joyner have won over crowds with revealing spandex creations that could be deemed as underwear – there certainly wasn't space to wear anything underneath. The hottest young stars of Wimbledon's Centre Court have kept pulses racing, too, with Russian goddess Anna Kournikova stepping out in the tightest hot pants known to mankind and the Williams sisters continuing to dazzle in miniscule rainbow-colored dresses and matching briefs. The butt-covering potential of the sports pant may well be lost for good.

And don't think that these once-frumpy underthings are still fashioned with most of the focus on function and little concern for style. Designers have realized that the tennis court and running track aren't actually that different from the catwalk, and Diane von Furstenberg has recently made the leap from couture to sportswear by creating snug hot pants (as well as dresses and tracksuits) for Reebok adorned with her famous Seventies prints. Yoga buffs like supermodel Christy Turlington, with her label Nula, have also transformed the dreary world of graying sports briefs. Yogis now show off smalls made from second-skin fabrics (generally revealed mid "downward dog") that are totally luxe – no nylon in sight! – supersoft Lycra, and stretchy jersey silks that feel good, preserve one's modesty, and miraculously look pretty attractive, too. But this isn't the only advancement in the sports department. Serious athletes who are looking for more than a style kick can now purchase underpants in thermal fabrics that draw away sweat (to keep you lovely and snug while mountain climbing/cross-country skiing/skidoo racing), or have additional pockets (for tennis balls or shuttlecocks). And go-faster stripes? They really work! (Okay, that's a lie, but scientists have to have something to work towards.)

And before this? The first athlete to show off her sporty smalls was featured in a mosaic found in Sicily, circa fourth century A.D.

Sports briefs may not look like much but, hot and sweaty, just the thought of them makes millions of men horny. Bring on those artificial fibers . . .

The woman is well-toned, wearing sporty briefs and a bra almost
identical to the kind women currently wear to the local gym; simple,
not showy, and well structured, gimmick-free.

Sports briefs have a cult following. American teen girls are
constantly searching for the hottest thing to wear while shaking
their pom-poms (currently boyshorts with "Spirit!" or "Cheer!"
emblazoned across the butt.) Then there's the teen boys, who are
equally as passionate about the cause. Sports briefs may not look like
much but, hot and sweaty, just the thought of them makes millions
of men horny. Bring on those artificial fibers . . .

SLOGGI

As the best-selling branded brief in the world, Sloggi are as proud as pants. Since 1978, Sloggi have sold 750 million pants and use enough stretch-edging in a year to wind 750 times the globe. Keeping the world's pants up is no mean feat.

Sloggi began when Triumph International patented a unique fabric called Corespun (cotton wrapped around Lycra thread), making some of the comfiest panties around.

From putting logos on waistbands, creating the Tai (a cross between a G-string and a "tanga" brief), and making pants as "bottom boosters," Sloggi have kept up with the changing trends of smalls. But the British public was outraged recently when Sloggi ran an advertisement featuring women in G-strings. Traffic-stopping, certainly, but the poster aroused such feeling in the U.K. that it was even torn from a billboard. Sloggi revels in its own infamy; just a year before, they ran a "Happy New Rear" advertisement featuring panty-clad female cyclists, shot from behind.

A touch of TV coverage hasn't done the brand any harm, either. England rugby star, Ben Cohen, admitted he had batches of Sloggi underwear shipped out to him when he was competing for the World Cup.

So what's the next trick up Sloggi's trouser leg? Well, the latest panty style – the Sloggi Sensation – is planned to take pant-land by storm, claiming to be the softest and most comfortable brief in the world. With a "60 percent finer stitch," the Sensation promises to keep one's body temperature balanced, so you'll be cosy when it's cold and cool when it's hot. Temperature-sensitive pants, anyone?

Thongs & G-strings

VPL: three seemingly harmless letters that strike fear into the heart of the fashion conscious. Their meaning? Visible Panty Line — or, in other words a major style *faux-pas* and social death to anyone with an ounce of vogue.

· · · · ● · · · ·

But let's break this down even further. A VPL is the underwear equivalent of spinach between the teeth; it doesn't matter how great you look because the offending panty line overshadows all else. For years women had to gulp and swallow this unsightly apparition; we would slip on a pair of white trousers knowing that our underwear was gleaming through the translucent fabric, or put on a slim skirt aware that the elegant line would be ruined by the butt/knicker interface.

Then one day, an answer; a discovery that was surely on a par with the contraceptive pill transformed women's lives. The thong — a revolutionary slip of fabric that fit snuggly between the butt cheeks and became invisible under clothes. The thong was a fashion revelation and men everywhere rejoiced in the display of the ripe, peachy globes of flesh known as the posterior. Lo, the thong was born!

The skinny strings can be traced back to the World Fair 1939 in the United States, when the New York Mayor, Fiorello LaGuardia, ordered the city's nude dancers to cover themselves up. The girls wanted to keep their bottoms bared, so the thong was the thing to cover their modesty (albeit only a small part.) Aptly, almost 60 years later, the Big Apple's nude dancers are still wearing thongs in strip clubs across the city.

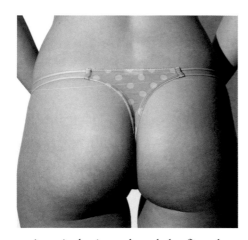

Though thongs were first aired at the end of the Thirties, they didn't take off at this time as they were considered risqué and inappropriate. The style reared its head again in 1974, courtesy of provocative Austrian fashion designer Rudi Gernreich. At the same time as showing a saucy frontless swimsuit, he introduced the first thong bikini. The public was underwhelmed. After all, it wasn't so long since knee-length shorts were worn for swimming, and although times had moved fast, American women weren't yet ready to display their booties on the beach.

Brazilian women, on the other hand, were only too thrilled to show off what God had given them. Called "tangas," their briefly cut bikini bottoms were all the rage on beaches from Ipanema to Rio De Janiero (perhaps explaining why South America became such a holiday hot spot in the late Seventies.) Was it the mojitos and mambo that attracted the tourists or the Brazilian babes with brown butt cheeks bouncing with every sandy step they took? (Unsurprisingly, a curvy behind is still considered essential in Brazilian culture and women are prepared to drop thousands on plastic surgery to create a J. Lo-style "bubble butt.")

The craze headed north and by the early 1980s American lingerie stores such as Frederick's of Hollywood and newcomer

Victoria's Secret started to stock the panties. It's hard to pinpoint exactly when almost every woman in the western world between the ages of 18 and 35 could say they owned a thong, but that's pretty much where we are today. Pant-land has been revolutionized – and, like Tom Cruise, Mel Gibson and so many of today's diminutive movie stars – it's often the smallest things that have the biggest impact.

"Let me see that thong!" crooned Dru Hill's Sisqo in his 2000 smash "The Thong Song." The video featured the 5ft 5in singer (another compact success story) surrounded by hundreds of women strutting their stuff in strings. Never before has a style of underwear sold so many records, or a pop single sold so much underwear. Stores across America reported an increase in thong sales when the track topped the charts.

But it hasn't stopped there – thongs are the darlings of the hip hop world and Sir Mix-A-Lot's "Baby Got Back" was a homage to the rounded rump (and had a video jam-packed with booty). Rap artists 2 Live Crew took the trend even further in the late Eighties when they decked out the stage with thonged-up women during their performance of the banned track "Me So Horny."

Although their fans were thrilled, the local authorities weren't, and three members of the group were arrested.

In the 1990s thongs were the fastest-growing segment of the US$2 billion-dollar underwear industry. Minor tweaks to the cut earned these skimpy panties different titles – from the thong, which has a one-inch strip of fabric down the back, to a G-string, which, as the name suggests, is more like a string of fabric akin to dental floss that goes across the hips and down the butt. Designers got creative, too, from crazily expensive thongs studded with diamonds and crystals to the pearl thong famously worn by Samantha in *Sex and the City*. This lacy number with the "string" made of the precious gems, gave a whole new meaning to the classic "twinset and pearls."

A VPL is the underwear equivalent of spinach between the teeth. Thongs are the answer.

But, as with everything that seems so good, there must be a downside – and thongs are no exception. The burden a thong-wearer often has to suffer is a constant, nagging discomfort. But you can learn to live with a wedgie like you do an annoying sibling; an ever-present irritant who is invading your personal space. And that's not the worst of it.

The other harrowing and all-out agonizing trend to be spawned by the thong is the invasive bikini wax, AKA "The Brazilian." Curling up into the fetal position while your own personal torturer smears searing hot wax between your butt cheeks and proceeds to rip away at your most intimate regions is a procedure that only the most fearless and dedicated of women will endure (then again, Posh Spice proclaims to be a fan).

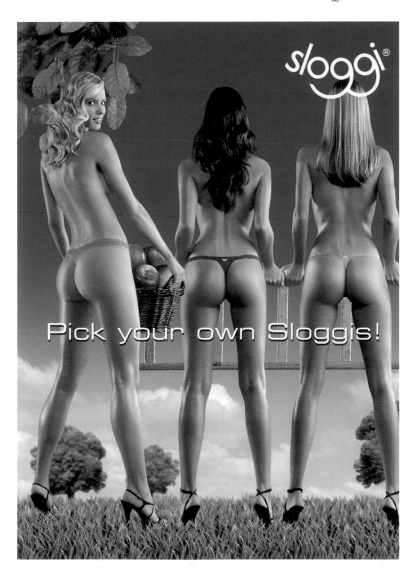

BARBARELLA

Director: Roger Vadim, 1968

Based on a classic French comic strip created in 1962, the psychedelic sci-fi/sex comedy *Barbarella* features a female space agent who encounters a whole host of aliens desperate to have sex with her. Obviously.

The character of Barbarella (played by workout queen Jane Fonda) is searching for the scientist, Duran Duran, who threatens to destroy the galaxy. Her task is to save the world.

But more important than the woolly plot, Barbarella has the most incredible collection of naughty, futuristic leather and PVC panties you've ever seen. Team those arousing pants with knee-high boots, body armour, tight gold suits, and a big blonde mane and she's a fantasy figure that is truly out of this world.

Designer Jacques Fonteray is responsible for the fetishistic costumes, and with such a fabulously frothy plot, almost every scene of Barbarella's escapades provides an excellent opportunity for her to strip to her pants. But in true Sixties sex-kitten style, she had the body for it.

Now that Jane Fonda is a political activist and has reached her golden years, it's unlikely you'll see her flashing her pants in the near future. So who's next to display her silver undies on the silver screen? Well, Drew Barrymore has promised to re-make the film, and will take the role of Barbarella herself. Since it is being written by John August (the guy responsible for *Charlie's Angels* and Cameron Diaz's infamous panty-dancing) there's sure to be more memorable underwear moments.

With no place for stray hairs to hide, the Nazi-style treatment of the spa world strips you of your fuzzy bits, and your dignity.

Recently, the charm of the thong has been wearing thin (a bit like the strings themselves.) And now that low-rise jeans have become the hottest thing on the market, the nation has seen one-too-many thongs peeking over the top of ultra-low trousers, though hats off to Gucci who did try to make this a fashion statement by producing strings with classy, interlocking letter "G"s on the side.

Celebs like Britney Spears, Tara Reid, and Pamela Anderson have revealed their dental-floss wedgies in so many paparazzi pics that what was once considered an intimate glimpse at a lady's underwear choice is now seen as sleazy and over-exposed. And although it cannot be denied that thongs do work best with slim-fitting clothes, after years of waxing and wedgies, women are looking for other, less masochistic options.

A curvy behind is still considered essential in Brazilian culture and women are prepared to drop thousands on plastic surgery to create a J. Lo-style "bubble butt".

The thong looks set to represent a generation, like the ra-ra skirt, the blow-wave, or flares, which have gone before them. They are a historical snapshot; revealing a time when women were prepared to do anything in the pursuit of beauty and sexual attraction (hey, like that's never happened before – anyone remember the corset?) And while there will be some women who find it hard to kiss these eye-watering knickers goodbye, others will be sighing with relief and running to the stores in pursuit of complete butt coverage.

"To be sexy, nudes need
a little underwear."

— Mason Cooley

COSABELLA

As a lingerie designer, there is no greater praise than A-listers singing the virtues of your thongs. In the hit film *Shallow Hal*, Gwyneth Paltrow wore a Cosabella chemise to match Jack Black's super-sized thong, created specially for his character.

Ugo Campello, who started the brand in 1983 with wife, Valeria, and partner, Sergio Oxman, is delighted to have their designs in the movies.

After all, Britney Spears was seen cavorting in the movie *Crossroads* wearing a Cosabella camisole and pants, and Jennifer Garner wore a Cosabella camisole in the film *Daredevil*. The Cosabella name has been dropped on *Sex and the City*, and fans include Sarah Jessica Parker, Uma Thurman, and Calista Flockhart.

Meaning "beautiful thing" in Italian, Cosabella started designing for hot, young women, corporate-lawyer-types and the wife who wants a super-sexy date with her husband. First stop was the thong. Regarded at the time as an uncomfortable necessity, they chose the thinnest fabric to make it almost non-existent. It took a lot to persuade the public to ditch their big panties: "Stores weren't ready for our tiny G-strings, but we went door-to-door convincing retailers that this was a big trend." Fortune was shining on Cosabella and their business went from strength to strength. Then, when waistbands started to go south, they jumped on the low-rider thong bandwagon and had trouble keeping up with demand.

"Cosabella is like a pungent Italian pasta," Oxman says, meaning that the racy look created by their tiny thongs is not for everyone. "But when it's good, it is very, very good."

Kitsch & Cute

Forget sexy or functional – wouldn't it be great if underwear were funny? If lifting *your* skirt would actually give *you* something to chuckle about. Like most other things in life, we tend to take our underwear too seriously. Enter: kitsch underpants.

· · · · ● ● ● · · ·

This style of smalls is one of those things in life that just makes you smile – it's the undergarment that fulfills your childhood fantasies. Wish you were a princess? Get a pair of pink knickers with your regal title written in rhinestones. Always wanted to be a super-hero? Then have your favorite caped crusader flying across your butt cheeks. Are you a tomboy condemned to floral and pastels? Now's your chance to wear bright blue Y-fronts.

But don't think that the fantasies are limited to pre-school. Kitsch pants also give you the chance to reveal your erotic desires without feeling like you're sharing too much. When cute boyshorts read "Eat Me!" "Saucy," or "Horny Mama," they are definitely more cool than corny, and phrases that would never pass a girl's lips can now be uttered with reckless abandon. Don't be surprised if these raunchy declarations actually turn men on. Suggestive comments have a knack of heating up foreplay by saying the things a woman is too coy to utter, and letting a guy know exactly what kind of woman lurks beneath the knickers. There's actually something surprisingly feminist about slogan briefs. Their to-the-point quips let a woman talk like a man, while still looking like a lady; they get a woman's own desires across and set her up for foreplay with mutual gains. They're provocative without being too lap-dancer and smart without being staid.

Snazzy emblems and sauce-speak somehow make cotton panties cool, hence the profusion of ironic undies to be found in mainstream stores. And real, sexy women are wearing them. Think of Cameron Diaz shaking her booty in the hit movie *Charlie's Angels*. The big surprise of the movie was not that the world's highest-paid actress could dance, but that she chose to cover her shapely bottom with Spiderman briefs while doing so. The A-list stylesetter provoked a fashion for comic-inspired briefs, but sadly, few could fit into the little boy's version like Cameron did. Luckily, manufacturers caught on and quickly reproduced the super-hero styles in adult sizes.

The term "kitsch panties" doesn't just refer to retro undergarments. Anything with bows, baubles, or a theme is encompassed by this description (a sports-inspired boyshort with a number emblazoned on the butt and footie-boot-inspired lacing up both sides, for example). When women want to be charmed, amused

and titillated by their underwear choices, they should check out underwear designers that specialize in sexy underwear with a tongue-in-cheek vibe. These cheeky styles can include panties that tie at the side with huge silk bows, have a "baby-doll" feel, or bottom-enhancing features, and while they don't exactly work under clothes, as bedroom wear they can be both amusing and adorable. Agent Provocateur has virtually cornered the market with their line in nursery-rhyme-inspired undies. Their hip-hugging knickers covered with frills make like Little Miss Muffet but the attached suspenders add a whole dollop of sauce to the fluffy confection.

Also more cute than kitsch, Strumpet & Pink are the silky, sexy-yet-innocent creations of Lisa Morgan and Melanie Probert, two artists who decided to set up a sideline in underwear. Pioneering the trend for handmade lingerie, their knickers are delicious creations of silk chiffon, crepe de chine, and cotton adorned with frills, ruffles, and ribbons. "Neither of us like matching sets," explains Lisa, "we were more interested in knickers and focusing on how a woman feels when she's wearing them."

The sexiness equated with kitsch underthings comes from the wearer's nonchalance. Like cotton briefs, the woman who chooses cute smalls isn't necessarily intending on the entire world seeing them – but that's sometimes what makes them even hotter. Remember Molly Ringwald in the 1984 cult classic *Sixteen Candles*? She probably didn't think her panties would be shown to the entire male population of her high school (for a dollar apiece) when she chose to wear a pair covered in cute little strawberries. Nor did she anticipate the cutesy briefs would end up in the hands of the school heart-throb. But, somehow, the fact that she was wearing them, instead of a hot lacy pair, meant that she and the briefs became even more charming.

Snazzy emblems and sauce-speak somehow make cotton panties cool, hence the profusion of ironic undies to be found in high-street stores.

So if a woman needs to bring a little sunshine into her life or rediscover her inner child she should splash out on a pair of funny, sexy, kitschy knickers. Or a kitsch-panty-wearer can spend the day chuckling to herself when she thinks about the sassy words scrawled across her butt. What better way to celebrate a favorite old TV show or comic book hero than by wearing their image on the tush? OK, so they're not chiffon or revealing, but sexiness comes in many different forms, and a sense of humor is always top of the list. This way every girl's butt gets to have the last laugh.

So they're not chiffon
or revealing, but sexiness
comes in many different
forms, and a sense of humor
is always top of the list. This
way your butt will be having
the last laugh.

HANTY PANTIES:
MAKE YOUR OWN PANTIES

A "Hanty" is a pair of panties fashioned from a handkerchief, as featured on Japanese pants designer Runo's website (www.max.hi-ho.jp/hotaru/panty). According to Runo, Japanese women have slim hips, so a simple handkerchief can cover them fine. Runo does have some problems with the name "panties," however.

"Why Hanty and not Hanties? Oh, I can't understand why 'panties' is plural. A friend says, 'Because panties have three holes.' But your nose has two holes. Do you have 'noses'? Anyway, Hanty was named by me."

What you need:

- A large handkerchief
- Thin cotton cloth as lining
- Lace
- Ribbon and trimmings
- Elastic
- Sewing kit or sewing machine

How to make a Hanty Panty:

- Print the pattern file from the Hanty Panty site on two sheets of A4 paper.
- Cut out each pattern. **1:** front. **2:** crotch. **3:** back.
- Put the front between two pieces of crotch and sew.
- Turn the crotch inside out and sew to the back cloth.
- Stitch from the outside.
- Sew the front and back at the sides.

The finishing touches:

- Sew a ribbon in a bow.
- Add embroidery, plastic jewels, and so on.
- Pass the elastic through into the waist and the hem.

PAUL FRANK

Kitsch, cute, and cool, Julius the monkey adorns bedrooms across the globe and has developed a cult following. A favorite with celebs, he has also been spotted winking from Cameron Diaz's handbag and Drew Barrymore's vest top.

Paul Frank took his influences from skatewear and American commercial art of the Fifties and Sixties to come up with his ideas – from his tighty-whitey thongs to the rock-your-socks fundi wear (fun + undies, geddit?).

He started out in 1995 hand-stitching wallets in a garage, now Paul Frank Industries employs 30 people with a $5million turnover. An even greater measure of his success are his recent collaborations with the likes of fellow kitsch-and-cute fashion giant Hello Kitty in 2002 and The King himself through E.P.E. (Elvis Presley Enterprises) in 2004.

With no formal design training, Frank took art classes after he left High School and made good use of a sewing machine his mum bought for him. He and his girlfriend at the time, Daiquiri, would draw animals on their notes to each other; one day he drew her a monkey based on a sock puppet his grandmother had once given to him. The monkey became Julius.

When a PR friend spotted the creative potential in Frank's designs he decided to set up the business. These days Frank makes appearances in stores and shops, autographing his clothes with a little monkey or giraffe and getting to know his audience. "They always seem excited. I guess the monkey makes people get a nice feeling inside. It reminds us of when we were little," he says.

Power Pants

Power pants made it big on the Seventies TV icon Wonder Woman. Those hip-hugging, hold-it-all-in briefs were the answer to every man's dreams. This was one powerful lady who was prepared to fight for justice – and had killer curves to boot.

· · · ● ● ● ● · · ·

But Linda Carter wasn't alone in redefining the oversized granny knicker as the sexiest duds on the planet. Seventies sisters the *Charlie's Angels*, with their butt-kicking prowess and skin-tight flares, plus *The Dukes of Hazard*'s Daisy Duke (clad in the shortest denim hot pants ever screened) were clearly holding everything in with a pair of stomach-reducing, bottom-enhancing briefs. Remember, this was the era of the flat belly and pert posterior and for those women who weren't blessed with these assets, nothing solved the problem like a pair of power pants – guaranteed to give you the rear you always thought you deserved.

Power pants can redefine a woman's shape and structure the body to create curves where they're wanted and hide them where they're not. Not for the fainthearted, power pants are worn by only the most fearless females – from Madonna's Blonde Ambition tour corsets to the early Nineties designer Thierry Mugler, who made intimate body armor into an art form. Strong women will always turn to a pair of knickers that can kick ass and they need to look no further than power pants.

Before they morphed into power pants, this style of underwear was known as a girdle, and before that, the closest thing was a corset. In fact, women brave enough to cram their bodies into constricting and redefining undergarments date back as far as 2000 B.C., evidenced by a Greek statue of a Cretan woman in a tight bodice that pushes her busom aloft and holds her stomach in.

The tales of torturous corsets have been well documented – from women in the 1400s and onwards having ribs broken by being laced in too tight, to losing unborn children thanks to the insistence of female corsetry even during pregnancy. So it's no surprise to learn that designers were constantly looking for ways to achieve that svelte figure without the use of tough whalebone.

In the 1900s, underwear designer Paul Poiret created a radical new style that ditched corsetry boning and replaced it with more flexible fabrics and paneling to achieve the desired figure. Despite the partial liberation from overly constrictive underthings, women were still chasing the dream body. In 1930, British *Vogue* declared, "No woman should have a bulge in her body," causing wannabe fashionistas to run to the stores and buy up anything that promised to hide their bulges. Most opted for the new all-in-one girdles with integral bra and panties that fitted like a second skin. It was around this time that the word "flattering" made it into the dictionary. Nowadays it's used to describe an item of clothing that makes the body look more attractive, but in the Thirties when flappers wanted to be boyishly flat – breasts, stomachs, and bottoms – the word "flattering" still meant a woman was looking good, but for quite different reasons.

By the Forties and Fifties woman were celebrating their curves again, so long as they were in the right places. Dior's "New Look" called for waspy waistlines that were accentuated by full skirts, and a decade on the circle skirts worn by swing

dancers called for the same slim middle. Roll-on girdles sat high above the navel with a special panel that covered and held in the stomach. Their constrictive nature was no doubt reassuring to parents whose daughters were out courting for the first time. Frankly speaking, there was no way a guy was getting inside those knickers.

And that's the irony of power pants – no matter how good you look to a man from the outside, once your outer layers of clothes are removed and you're down to your undies, the wind can suddenly go from his sails. Because, the truth is, there's nothing remotely attractive about a woman who has crammed herself into a pair of flesh-colored granny pants. The whole image resembles a badly stuffed sausage. And the knickers may look bad, but trying to get them off is even more of a passion killer. Remember the lovable rogue, Daniel Cleaver, from *Bridget Jones's Diary*, played by Hugh Grant? He seduced La Singleton, only to get her home and find that she'd worn her granny knickers, her apple catchers, her power pants. It goes without saying she hadn't expected to end up in bed with him (durr...who would wear big pants if they did?) but she still found herself in a dilemma. We winced in sympathy as we watched her struggle out of them, knowing that, after an entire night in those knickers, her bottom would have more wrinkles than a Sharpei.

Despite the downsides, women still love power pants. It's partly a control thing; in an era when women can let it all hang out if they want to, there's something enticingly retro and regimented about squeezing into a pair of snug tummy-warmers that give the body a girl's always wanted. And with the revival of 1950s fashion, and designers from Prada to Moschino showing full skirts and tea dresses on their catwalks, there's never been a better time for women to become reacquainted with their waist.

"Big knickers are back. The thong is gone."
– Kylie Minogue

These days power pants can remedy every figure complaint. If a girl hates her stomach she can get a pair with a flattening panel. Are saddlebags your problem? A knee-length body-shaper will do the trick. Want Beyoncé's bottom? Look no further than pants with a padded rear. There are even styles with added up-lift boosters for the bum.

BRIDGET JONES'S DIARY

Director: Sharon Maguire, 2001

The scatty diarist Bridget Jones opted for her big pants over a teeny G-string for her date with boss, Daniel Cleaver. Little did she know that things would get steamy at her apartment later that evening. Cue those immortal lines in movie history:

Daniel: "Now, these are very silly little boots, Jones. And this is a very silly little dress. And um, these are . . . f*** me, absolutely enormous pants!"
Bridget: "Jesus, f***!"
Daniel: "No no, don't apologise; I like them. Hello Mummy!"

Gargantuan knickers are unlikely to turn a man into a raging beast, but, incredibly, that's just what they do for Hugh Grant's character, Daniel. Cinema-goers flocked to see the movie, but no one realised that such a momentous event in pant history was happening right before their eyes. Hollywood superstar Renee Zellweger had eaten her way to a wobbly size 12 to play the role, and donned the flesh-colored bloomers to disguise her protruding tummy. It wasn't attractive, nor was it likely to start a trend, yet in a recent on-line survey the *Bridget Jones's Diary* "big pants scene" was voted the Number One Movie Moment.

Nowadays, the words "big pants" have become synonymous with Bridget Jones, and these capacious undies have made a massive comeback. British chain Marks & Spencer, source of all panty-knowledge, claim: "Since the launch of *Bridget Jones's Diary*, sales of big pants have

soared. They used to be associated with your grandma, but that's all changed. Now they are high fashion." Yep, belly-warmers are back in vogue.

Almost a quarter of 25 to 34-year-old women readily admit to buying tummy-toning knickers. And once the public started coming out of the closet, the celebs did, too. Geri Halliwell admitted that at the height of her Spice Girls fame she was a fan of tummy controllers, and wore a pair under the infamous red-sequinned dress at the Brit Awards ceremony during the Spice Girl's reign.

It seems like Oscar-nominated Renee will never quite be able to escape the pants furore.

Last year she was reported to be furious when two pairs of her ultra-sexy La Perla knickers were lost in a west Hollywood laundry. This is shocking news: we can reveal here that the leader of the big pants revolution is actually a sexy-knicker-wearing traitor.

They are the Wonderbra of the knicker world. And it's not just mere mortals who turn to power pants as a confidence-booster – a pregnant Gwyneth Paltrow once flashed her black knee-length spandex pants from under her Calvin Klein dress at an awards show in Vegas.

The other reason women are smitten with power pants is comfort. Today pants don't have to be made with a suck-it-all-in fabric, they can just be . . . well, big. What bliss to forget about wedgies, high-cut legs or low-cut waistbands because you're wearing a pair of knickers that cover it all – a pair your granny would be proud of.

> There's something enticingly retro about squeezing into a pair of snug briefs that give you the body you've always wanted.

And the best news yet? Big pants might just be cool again. According to Kylie Minogue, pop princess and underwear designer extraordinaire, thongs are so over and big is better: "Big knickers are back. Women want comfort again – and I don't mean the sort of underwear our grandmothers wore. It'll be more French and sexy. The thong is gone." Big, comfy, sexy knickers – now that's what women want.

Power pants will never die, they are always being reinvented and paid homage to. They're what a woman wears when she wants to make a statement about domination. Powerful panties on the inside make powerful personalities on the outside. Our power role models include Madonna, Courtney Love, and Xena, Warrior Princess. And let's face it, could sassy Seventies icon Wonder Woman really have saved the world from evil in anything else?

PLAYTEX

Tummy-control underpants have taken over where corsets left off. Big knickers might be trendy, but tummy-controllers can be a different breed. The main difference? They're designed to make women look good in their clothes, rather than out of them.

A true underwear giant, Sara Lee Corp. owns labels such as Playtex, Bali, Glamorise, and Just My Size. Based in Chicago, the company was originally called Sara Lee Kitchens, when bakery founder Charles Lubin named it after his daughter, Sara Lee.

Sara Lee boasts ownership of America's number one best-selling stretchy brief, the Skimp Skamp by Bali, a deeply unsexy but comfy number. Clearly, the pink champagne to mocha and moonlight colors appeal to the masses, as does the $5 price tag. Bali sells specific control panties, such as the briefly named "Powershape Firm Control Lace Shapewear Thigh Slimmer." But forget this style if you aim to show off your cute belly-button piercings in low-rise jeans.

The Sara Lee label Just My Size uses the slogan "Beauty is what happens when you're busy being yourself." Provided a girl can still breathe in their firm control pants. Famous for its recent "Beauty on the Move" tour, Just My Size traveled to more than 90 US Wal-Mart stores inviting customers to board an 18-wheeler truck for a shopping experience like no other. It began with a questionnaire that the customer inserted into a scanner to establish their body shape: apple, pear, hourglass, or rectangle. Armed with this information a lady could determine her panty size and which style of Just My Size underwear would best flatter a particular figure, size, or shape.

Upping the glam stakes, the Sara Lee label, Playtex, was responsible for the Wonderbra adverts featuring voluptuous blonde Eva Herzigova and the slogans "Hello boys!" and "Or are you just pleased to see me?" However, Playtex has an embarrassing little sister called "I Can't Believe It's a Girdle!" Funnily enough, the girdle doesn't get the same kind of billboard coverage. It claims to tone the tummy, slim the thighs, and even has garter tabs so girls can wear stockings over their long pants.

As the proud owners of the isometric Body Briefer, Glamorise is star of Sara Lee inventions. Designed for "active lifestyles," the patented isometric construction and four-way stretch is supposed to feel like being on the end of an all-day massage. Sounds good, but wear it in the long leg style, and even the Victorians might think a woman was overdressed.

Va-Va-Voom

Some lingerie just screams to be seen. Imagine sashaying down a catwalk in turquoise tulle, lavender lace, scarlet silk, or even champagne chiffon, featuring tiny bows, touchable beads, and vintage boning. In va-va-voom panties women feel like sex on legs.

· · · · · ● ● · · · ·

And while we're on the subject, sex and underwear are so intrinsically linked that they almost have a chicken-and-egg quality. Were women created with their genitals hidden inside, just to make them more exciting when revealed? Are women repeating that same process when they wear arousing undergarments? Did Eve cover her most intimate bits with a fig leaf, just to make them more mysterious and alluring to Adam? Let's face it, leaving something to the imagination is heaps more tantalizing than having everything on show, and the gauzy fabrics and cunningly placed peepholes of va-va-voom underwear give tempting glimpses of what's underneath.

From ancient times, part of the desire for women to wear undergarments has been to give their bodies a more attractive shape and silhouette, but the other reason has been to differentiate their figures from the opposite sex – cue sensuous fabrics and embellishments, uplifting bras, and butt-enhancing briefs. Women wanted men to remember that under their clothes they look oh-so-different.

The corsets, the frilly silk bloomers, the satin stockings were all womanly plumage; all part of the underwear arsenal that women used to decorate the body parts that men fantasized over. Because as long as there have been men and women, there have been men craving women's bodies. Back in the 1700s when the opportunity to unlace a lady's corset was rare, men developed ankle and foot fetishes instead. It was, after all, the only part of a female body they got to see long enough to lust after – such was their desire for the opposite sex . . .

Femmes fatales have long used va-va-voom panties to seduce men. In fact, even when women were supposed to be "proper" and adhere to strict moral codes (when holding hands with a man was only a step away from promiscuity), there were always a few brazen babes willing to reveal some flesh and shake things up a bit. The French seemed to have the edge when it came to sleaze. They were the originators of cabaret and the art of striptease, with nineteenth-century acts like *Coucher d'Yvette* in Paris (a favorite of Toulouse-Lautrec). These women knew how to reduce men to drooling idiots. They aroused and excited the crowd with their exotic, decadent underwear, which they slowly, teasingly, removed piece by piece. Think Marlene Dietrich and her saucy strip in the 1930s movie *The Blue Angel,* or Liza Minelli and the women of the Kit Kat Club in the film *Cabaret.*

> Panties had to arouse the audience with see-through, silky designs that men fantasized about their wives wearing at home.

These were not subversive females, unhappy with how they made a living. They were bawdy, brazen, and sensuous, using their sexuality to make a pretty penny. Naturally, racy underwear was essential to the act. Panties had to arouse the audience with see-through, silky designs that men fantasized about their wives wearing at home (though they never would, since back then risqué women who dressed like this were untouchable).

Even more out of reach were the pin-up girls of the 1940s – movie stars like Rita Hayworth and Jean Harlow – and models celebrated by the artist Vargas. They posed provocatively in French knickers and pointy bras and became a symbol of hope and freedom to American soldiers, who painted their images on their fighter planes and carried pictures of them under their helmets.

When the war was over maybe it was the delight of finally having their men home and the need to procreate (and fast), or perhaps the desire to be a "perfect wife" really did mean becoming a cook in the kitchen and a whore in the bedroom, but by the 1950s, striptease suddenly became mainstream. Burlesque was the hottest new thing in America and housewives could take classes to learn how to strip correctly for their husbands.

Naturally, the increase in striptease opportunities also meant a greater demand for va-va-voom underwear to show off. Now it wasn't just acceptable for women to wear sexy undergarments, it was positively encouraged. Celebrating your sexuality was all the rage, and movies like *La Dolce Vita* and the French flick *La Dénonciation* included the now-requisite striptease scene. From this time onwards, actresses have clamored to show off their striptease skills to varying degrees of success. Sophia Loren earned herself an A for her classy attempt in 1963's *Yesterday, Today and Tomorrow*, whereas Demi Moore's on-stage version in the 1996 flop *Striptease* was more like a D.

Nowadays women don't need to be strippers to splurge on racy panties. In fact teh line between erotic underwear and everyday styles has become so blurred that stores like the notoriously sexy Agent Provocateur hangs crotchless panties next to lace thongs and boyshorts.

Like an instant pick-me-up, slipping into glamorous underwear is a confidence-booster – no matter who else gets to see it. But right now, it's all about showing it off, anyway. The recent trend for underwear as outerwear has been sparked by the desire to flash a woman's sexy lingerie. Designers Jean Paul Gaultier and Vivienne Westwood have built their careers on corset-inspired tops, and Stella McCartney and Proenza Schouler recently revived the trend, proving that a silk camisole is *the thing* with jeans and a blazer.

Whereas underwear was once discreet and invisible, now women are simply itching to flash our bra straps or the logo-ed waistband of their briefs. Hip designer Deborah Marquit has made lace lingerie sets in fluorescent shades of green, orange, and pink that command to be seen peeking out from beneath a tank top – and *Sex and the City*'s SJP helped launch the trend on-screen when Carrie Bradshaw showed off her black skimpies from underneath a white tank top and skirt.

Forget the rent – there really is no better investment for women than a killer set of lingerie. Trust me when I say that a pair of frilly chiffon briefs that make the butt look extra pert (especially when worn with a pair of four-inch heels) are a better aphrodisiac than champagne and oysters. Girls should see their favorite pair of pulling pants like a lucky charm; whenever they have them on, you become a vamp – sexy, seductive, and empowered. It's funny how a small wisp of fabric can transform an entire character, from mild to wild, meek to magnificent. Girls should never *ever* underestimate the power of va-va-voom panties, and they should make sure they have a pair to slip into at all times.

DAMARIS

"Everyone's got good bum cleavage," insists 28-year-old London-based underwear designer Damaris Evans. Since starting her panties label she has created a frenzy for bow-tied and bejeweled knickers.

Cut like a Sixties bikini, the kinky little numbers have a peephole in the back, tied with a huge satin ribbon intended to hang out the back of your jeans. Her bestseller is the "corseted" knicker. "I don't agree with the no-VPL rule," she says. "My corset knickers lace up across the bum and seeing that criss-cross through a tight pencil skirt is very sexy. I wear them under floaty summer dresses all the time."

When Damaris was at college she started to make knickers for the dresses she'd designed — she soon decided that the pants were more fun than the outfits themselves. Fabric-wise, she was inspired by *Gone With the Wind*. "All the dresses in the film were lined with silk, not nylon," she explains. "Although it cost them a small fortune, the director wanted the actresses to feel amazing from the inside. I loved that idea."

Kate Moss, Kirsten Dunst, and Pamela Anderson have all invested in her cheeky creations. "Damaris underwear is like couture, the kind of thing you could get married in," explains model Liberty Ross. "Even if you're hungover, you feel great if you've got a good pair of knickers on."

The label is set to go from strength to strength with UK department store House of Fraser stocking a Damaris diffusion line, Mimi Holliday (her "porn star name," comprised of the name of her first pet plus her mother's maiden name!)

Fetish Fashion

What lurks in the depths of a woman's underwear drawer? Perhaps a little PVC number without a crotch? Fetishwear has become so popular that it's only a matter of time before the big chain stores stock vinyl thongs in three-packs.

• • • • ● ● • • •

Perhaps we have Catwoman to thank for our open-minded attitude to fetish fashion; the *Batman* femme fatale of 1966 was one of the first people in mainstream society to dress head-to-toe in PVC and get away with it. Of course, behind closed doors people had been getting their kicks from rubber, leather, whips, chains, and handcuffs for years, but until the caped crusader and his feline foe hit our screens, it was considered strange, perverted, and even dirty to adorn your body in this way to satisfy your sexual kink.

Fetishism is described in the dictionary as "the compulsive use of some object or part of the body as a stimulus in the course of attaining sexual gratification", and with panties covering the most intimate of body parts it's no wonder they're a main focus for fetishists. The options available to deck out intimate bits are unfathomable – think zips and whips, leather, leashes, and lacing, chains to attach to your piercings, lattice work, feathers, fur, and fringing. Women can choose from the low-rise rubber panty that barely conceals the butt crack, to the high-cut vinyl thong that is barely there at all. Or a crotchless pair for easy access to be strapped and locked in for complete submission.

Ironically, the chastity belt could be considered the first form of fetish fashion. Known as the "Venus belt" in ancient mythology (named after the goddess of love, herself), these metal briefs were an iron-clad assurance against adultery. Common during the Middle Ages, they were built at a husband's behest and decorated with precious jewels to signify his social status. The belt locked at the front and the husband – who was fighting a battle somewhere and probably raping and pillaging along the way – took the key with him to deter amorous advances from other men in his absence. For those who like to feel dominated, the chastity belt still holds a lot of allure; the uncomfortable metal digging into soft flesh just enhances the experience for those who like a little pain with their pleasure. And if the version from the 1400s doesn't turn you on, how about playing dress-up as Princess Leia in *Return of the Jedi*? Ah yes, despite the crisis in the galaxy, Princess Leia still managed to look a million dollars in her fabulous gold Venus belt and ankle cuff.

Make your choice from the low-rise rubber panty that barely conceals your butt crack, to the high-cut vinyl thong that is barely there at all.

Chastity belts developed a cult following by the nineteenth century, but the trend went underground. French Belle Époque jewelers designed bejeweled knickers and chastity belts, bought up by the Bourgeoisie and worn in the bedroom only. By the roaring Twenties, sadomasochism was rife in the sexual underworld and the chastity belt had been modified to a G-string with a padlock, accessorized once more with bondage-style whips, leather, and chains.

The corset also earned a place in the fetishist's lingerie drawer, and despite its original invention as a tool to enhance and flatter the feminine figure, it also became a symbol of power and superiority –

a must for any dominatrix. The queen of pop, Madonna – a huge fan of getting the public's knickers in a twist with her overtly sexual antics – had French designer Jean Paul Gaultier create a whole line of dominatrix-style "bullet cone" corsets for her Blonde Ambition tour. Seeing the material girl in satin corset, panties, sky-high heels, and a hand-held whip dominating her PVC-clad male dancers somehow made fetish fashion not only cool, but a seriously desirable pastime.

As fetishist's kinks kept getting kinkier, as they looked for more extreme ways to gets their rocks off, their dark, erotic underworld somehow came into the spotlight. Even before Catwoman in her skin-tight black leather, killer heels, and mask, there was Emma Peel – the classy Brit detective from the 1961 TV show *The Avengers*. She may have been the epitome of a lady, but her black leather one-piece was actually modeled on an actual fetish costume.

The 1960s brought with them free love and open minds, so the public not only became more responsive to these illicit underwear choices, they actually embraced them. British designer, Vivienne Westwood took inspiration from fetishists when she

Even before Catwoman, in her skin-tight black leather, killer heels and mask, there was Emma Peel – the classy Brit detective from the TV show *The Avengers*.

created the PVC and rubber punk collection for her Carnaby Street "Sex" shop in the 1970s. She was one of the first people to make underwear that would be worn as outerwear. The legendary Village People also played their part in bringing pervy fashion to the people with their "gay leather man" who told us it was fun to stay at the Y-M-C-A while strutting his stuff in a leather cap, braces, and chains. Surely someone appearing so regularly on our TV screens couldn't be into kinky sex – could he?

Sex shops, once considered seedy, run by leering, middle-aged men and reached down dark, back alleys also got a makeover. They became women-friendly, painted in pretty shades, and merchandise was laid out to look like a racier version of America's sex emporia, Victoria's Secret. The British high street chain Ann Summers opened its first store in Bristol in 1972 with the aim of spicing up the sex life of the masses. Ms Summers was already heating things up inside our homes, as horny housewives ditched Tupperware parties in favor of racy Ann Summers' get-togethers involving a few bottles of Lambrusco and a lot of squealing over sexy panties and toys. They sold lace

It took a while for people to accept sexwear and toys being sold freely on their high streets, but sex stores these days are almost as prevalent as Starbucks.

lingerie in a multitude of pastel shades that looked innocent enough until you clocked it had no crotch, and S&M kits for beginners that would heat up the average sex life without leaving you too badly burned in the process. It took a while for people to accept fetishwear and sex toys being sold freely on their high streets, but sex stores these days are almost as prevalent as Starbucks. (Well, we can dream.)

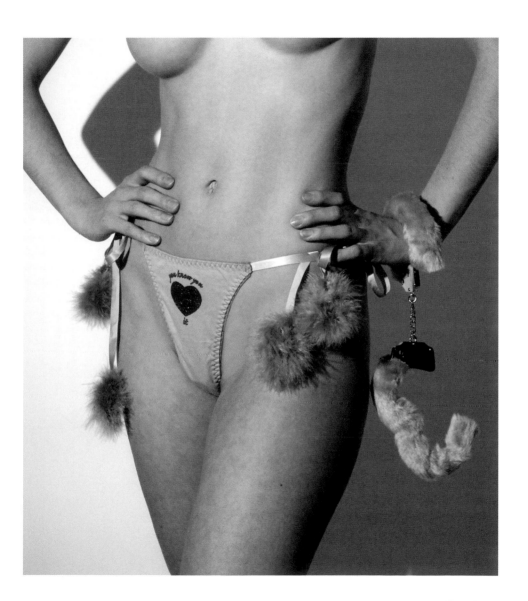

"The male is a domestic animal which, if treated with firmness and kindness, can be trained to do most things."

— Jilly Cooper

And, as always, the demand for something different has spawned another generation of new options. For the more discerning fetishist of London town, the sex-lover's emporium, Agent Provocateur, offers a decadent array of goods, while downtown New Yorkers can get their fix from the hip sex shop chain Babes in Toyland.

Meanwhile, on the West coast, Fredericks of Hollywood have been creating sensationally delicious underthings for quite some time. No one would have thought World War II would provide inspiration for such kind of lingerie, but when Frederick Mellinger returned from the front line in 1946, he brought with him the idea of selling a sensuous style of European lingerie to American women. At a time when good girls only wore pure, white cotton panties, they were blown away by his raunchy black undergarments.

From the Seventies *Playboy* image of the fiercesome Brigitte Nielson dripping in chains to Kylie, Britney, and Christina making PVC, vinyl, and leather the material of choice for their pop-video costumes, fetish fashion has become the norm. Just think about it: society has almost come a full circle – crotchless panties, once the only option for nineteenth-century women, are now readily available again – and no one's going to bat an eyelid when you buy them.

Okay, so maybe the average woman on the street still won't be rushing home to dress up in handcuffs, padlocks, and a PVC mask, but you can never tell if she's wearing a leather thong, a peephole bra, or a pair of crotchless panties underneath that smart and conservative business suit . . . But that's the beauty of fetish underwear – you can keep your kinky, pervy self private, because only you really need to know what turns you on.

AGENT PROVOCATEUR

Probably the most decadent panties in the world can be found at Agent Provocateur, the brainchild of Joseph Corré (son of eccentric British fashionista Vivienne Westwood and former Sex Pistols manager, Malcolm McClaren) and his wife, Serena Rees.

When the first Agent Provocateur boutique opened in London in 1994 it was a roaring success and was soon followed by a mail-order company and locations in New York and Los Angeles. Their aim is to make panties to promote "a sexy, super-hero feeling." Their high-priced designs — which are part-Moulin Rouge, part-sexy slapstick but all-woman — should "enchant and arouse wearers and their partners."

The ad campaigns for Agent Provocateur have become almost as legendary as the panties themselves — slogans like "A gentleman is expected to rise when a lady enters the room," and the infamously saucy ad featuring Kylie riding rodeo have made the label sizzling hot. One ingenious publicity stunt featured Naomi Campbell doing a striptease in the AP shop window.

But their ultimate coup has been to design an exclusive collection, named Salon Rose, for the British underwear institution Marks & Spencer. Strings, suspenders, and basques have the sexy stamp of Agent Provocateur, at a price any woman can afford. The shared vision of Rees and Corré is "to provide inspiration for desires that have been repressed by years of white cotton conservatism." With their turquoise tulle flying off M&S shelves faster than a cancan dancer's garter, they could almost be there.

Celebrity Panties

To date it seems that stars known for their fabulous bodies have seen panty designing as a natural career progression, so maybe it's a no-brainer that Elle Macpherson, Jennifer Lopez, and Kylie Minogue would look to their natural assets for inspiration.

· · · · · ● · · · ·

And they're not the only stars to have made their mark on the underwear industry; infamous Hollywood madame Heidi Fleiss has a line of sports briefs, Brit actress Sadie Frost has teamed with buddy Jemima French to design hip undies under the FrostFrench label, and even the richest teens in showbiz, Mary-Kate and Ashley Olsen, have a range of underwear in their empire.

So why succumb to knickers? Kylie says her Love Kylie range was inspired by a stint modeling underwear for Agent Provocateur. The actress-turned-singer kicked up a storm in a racy ad for the luxe lingerie company when she rode rodeo in suspenders and a push-up bra. Her infamous tush – which has probably received more praise than her voice and has revived her pop career with its starring role in her "Spinning Around" video – was undoubtedly another contributing factor. "It just seemed that I was linked with lingerie anyway, so why not take the step further and have my own range," said the star.

The styles exhibit the same attributes as the petite pop star herself: cheeky, fresh, and sexy. With names like Diva, Vamp, and Fever, they are an assortment of florals, bright shades of lace, and bad-girl black satin pieces. Kylie, who designs the line with her long-time stylist, William Baker, made our jaws drop when she was snapped in an ad for the collection astride a giant, rocket-shaped lollipop.

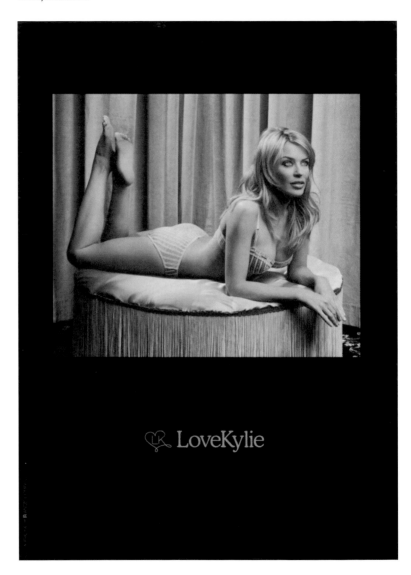

At press events she cleverly creates a stir by arriving with a bunch of
models clad only in Love Kylie lingerie and macs. Inevitably, the macs
are removed and cause a sensation.

The Aussie star recently commented that she'd like to draw
attention away from her infamous posterior. She's decided that, at age
34, she's too old to be showing it off and has ditched her signature hot
pants in favor of slinky dresses. Whether hiding her own asset will
affect her fashion assets remains to be seen, but the multimillionaire
whose collection currently sells in England, America, and Australia
seems to be lucky, lucky, lucky so far.

Jennifer Lopez, the owner of America's most famous bottom,
has recently added a lingerie line to her own empire. J. Lo already has

a successful clothing collection, range of jewelry and two fragrances to her name, but underwear does seem the natural choice. After all, she's never been afraid of showing off her best asset. During many of her music videos she appears in panties or a bikini and makes no secret of the hours she sweats in the gym to get her million-dollar curves.

Her lingerie range, J. Lo by Jennifer Lopez, is for women who want to dress like the star. The designs are a typical La Lopez cocktail of sexy and feminine with a sprinkling of bling. Think leopard-print cami-knickers trimmed with bright pink lace, or a pale peach thong with a rhinestone logo.

And the girl with curves hasn't forgotten her . . . er, more shapely sisters – the collection also features a line of power pants with stomach-

reducing and butt-lifting capabilities. Now anyone can get the famous J. Lo body without forking out for the personal trainer.

Like Kylie, Jennifer Lopez worked closely with her design team to set up the company, sending weekly parcels of fabrics and designs that she stumbled upon while touring the world and that she wanted to incorporate into her own line. Was she pleased with the result? You bet – she requested one of everything that was made – presumably so she can wear them while hanging "on the block."

As one of the world's hottest lingerie models, Elle "The Body" Macpherson knew better than most about how panties should fit before launching her own line, Elle

Elle's collection has struck gold; her simple designs appeal to no-nonsense Aussies.

Macpherson Intimates. She struck gold at home in Australia, where the supermodel's simple designs appeal to no-nonsense Aussies.

With spandex G-strings and bras as the mainstay of her collection, she had the market cornered, but perhaps the success of fellow-Aussie Kylie's racy line caused Elle to sex things up a bit. Now the collection features the same high-fashion, high-sauce concepts as Love Kylie and the companies are level pegging in many department stores.

However, in an attempt to up the sex stakes, Elle's ad campaign took things a step too far when a provocative print ad that ran in British *Vogue* was banned after complaints that it was way too explicit. The ad in question showed a keyhole view of a model clad only in a bra and knickers, with her thumbs pushed down the front of her panties. Macpherson argued that the intimate moment was inspired by the classic 1954 Alfred Hitchcock movie *Rear Window*, but the British Advertising Standards Authority was unmoved and banned the saucy advertisement anyway.

Naturally, sex plays a bit part in the success of a lingerie line, but stars know there's a fine line to tread between sexy and sleazy. Heidi Fleiss – all too often on the wrong side of that divide surprisingly

tackled the demure and dull world of the sports brief for her own foray into undergarments. HeidiWear is the last thing you'd expect from the former brothel owner, but this ex-con now insists she's playing it straight – and you don't get much straighter than cotton smalls.

The FrostFrench collection embodies everything that's cool about England: nostalgic prints, retro patterns, and a tongue-in-cheek humor – from cute pockets to clever ties. Their pants are casual, easy-to-wear pieces that are sexy in an uncontrived way. Scarlett Johansson stars in the movie *Lost in Translation* wearing a pair of their gauzy, granny knickers teamed with a cashmere sweater while mooching around the apartment, lending an air of uncomplicated sexiness that a lace thong could never provide.

FrostFrench embodies everything that is cool about England: nostalgic prints, retro patterns, and tongue-in-cheek humor.

The designers, Sadie Frost and Jemima French, stay firmly on the hip radar thanks to celeb pals who either model their designs or sit front row at their shows. They also celebrate their innate Britishness by offering afternoon tea in vintage china at their fashion shows.

Celeb designers are cashing in on their fame by creating their own lingerie lines, but the proof of the pudding lies in the tasting, and even if girls can't acquire J. Lo's curves or Kylie's cute butt by stepping into their signature smalls, will the styles be hot enough to keep them happy nevertheless? So far so good, but women should watch out for the next bright young thing with an urge to get them out of their knickers . . . and into their brand!

FROSTFRENCH

FrostFrench – the fashion label owned and run by Sadie Frost and Jemima French – is known for its gorgeous pants. Launched in 1999, FrostFrench began with mail-order scented knickers that Jemima dyed in huge vats in her back garden.

The label is known today for its sexy little knickers and camisoles, splattered with tongue-in-cheek prints and diamanté slogans. "We started doing this at the time when the lingerie market was all about lacy stuff and high-cut knickers, which I just hate," said Sadie. "We wanted to make them more fun, with Fifties cuts and funny prints." Focused on fun, one of their earlier designs was a pair of "kitten knickers." The kitten's ears are designed to peep out above the waistband of a low-slung pair of jeans and make a purring noise when you press them.

Neither Frost nor French are trained designers, so they work closely with their pattern-cutter to come up with ideas and drawings, as well as source much of the fabric. Celebrity friends helped raise their profile and now FrostFrench doubles its sales each season, thanks partly to Sadie's star pulling power, which can command headlines, and models such as Liberty Ross, Helena Christensen, and Jerry Hall. Even Kate Moss agreed to do a striptease on the catwalk.

FrostFrench are looking at franchising, particularly in Japan, where the label has achieved cult status. Back home in the UK, they continue to sell through a range of stores, including Selfridges, and have developed a diffusion range for Debenhams called Floozie. As for the future, they plan to crack America and open their own boutique in London.

Acknowledgements

The Publishers would like to thank the following companies for their generous assistance supplying pictures and samples: Agent Provocateur, Anne Summers, Bonds, Cosabella, Damaris, FrostFrench, Gap, La Perla, Marks & Spencer, Paul Frank, Rinko Uno, Sara Lee, Sloggi, Strumpet & Pink

Picture Credits